RELIGION AROUND THE WORLD

A CURIOUS KID'S GUIDE TO THE WORLD'S GREAT FAITHS

BY SONJA HAGANDER, MATTHEW MARUGGI, AND MEGAN BORGERT-SPANIOL
ILLUSTRATED BY CHESTER BENTLEY

beaming
books

MINNEAPOLIS

28 27 26 25 24 23 22   1 2 3 4 5 6 7 8

Hardcover ISBN: 978-1-5064-7013-9
Ebook ISBN: 978-1-5064-7116-7

Peer reviewers: Amy Allocco, Wendy Goldberg, Bussho Lahn, Chris Stedman, Maheen Zaman
"My Faith in My Words" youth contributors: Anna, Anya, Hafsa, Soren, Ved

Library of Congress Cataloging-in-Publication Data

Names: Hagander, Sonja, author. | Maruggi, Matthew, author. |
   Borgert-Spaniol, Megan, 1989- author. | Bentley, Chester, illustrator.
Title: Religion around the world : a curious kid's guide to the world's
   great faiths / by Sonja Hagander, Matthew Maruggi, and Megan
   Borgert-Spaniol ; illustrated by Chester Bentley.
Description: Minneapolis, MN : Beaming Books, 2022. | Series: Curious kids'
   guides | Audience: Ages 8-12 | Summary: "Religion around the World: A
   Curious Kid's Guide to the World's Great Faiths explores the world's
   major religious traditions, making the traditions, beliefs, practices,
   and history of each accessible to kids ages 8-12"-- Provided by
   publisher.
Identifiers: LCCN 2021058109 (print) | LCCN 2021058110 (ebook) | ISBN
   9781506470139 (hardcover) | ISBN 9781506471167 (ebook)
Subjects: LCSH: Religions--Juvenile literature.
Classification: LCC BL92 .H34 2022 (print) | LCC BL92 (ebook) | DDC
   200--dc23/eng20220314
LC record available at https://lccn.loc.gov/2021058109
LC ebook record available at https://lccn.loc.gov/2021058110

VN0004589; 9781506470139; JUN2022

Beaming Books
PO Box 1209
Minneapolis, MN 55440-1209
Beamingbooks.com

TABLE OF CONTENTS

INTRODUCTION

This is a book about religion around the world. The focus will be on the five most influential religions. These are Hinduism, Buddhism, Judaism, Christianity, and Islam. Nearly 80 percent of the world's population practices one of these religions. That's a lot of people!

But there are a ton of religions in the world. Have you heard of Jainism, Taoism, Shintoism, or Sikhism? These religions originate in South and East Asia. There are also folk religions. These are the spiritual beliefs and ways of life particular to distinct groups of people, such as tribes throughout Africa, Aboriginal Australians, and Indigenous people of North America. We'll explore some of these religions in this book too.

- ■ Buddhism
- ■ Christianity
- ■ Hinduism
- ■ Judaism
- ■ Islam
- □ No Clear Majority
- ■ Unaffiliated

Pew Research Center's Forum on Religion & Public Life, Global Religious Landscape, December 2012

Check out this map to see which religions are most common in different parts of the world.

Maps tend to show clean and simple borders. But religion is far from simple. Some people are born into one religion but grow up to choose another. Some people practice more than one religion at the same time. Other people don't practice any religion. When we stay curious, we can come to understand and appreciate what's unfamiliar. And that can only lead to good things.

Why are there so many religions? Why do people practice (or not practice) religion? And why does religion even matter?

These are big questions. Let's start with a (not really) small question. What *is* religion?

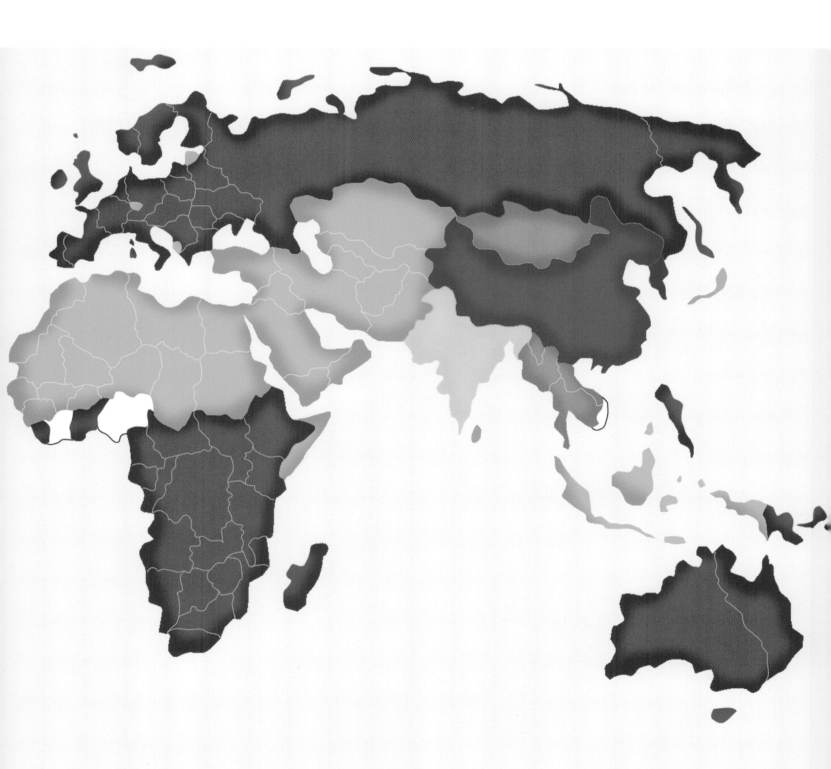

WHAT IS RELIGION?

Let's start with the word itself. *Religion* comes from the Latin word *religare*, which means "to bind or tie together again." This is what religion does. It binds together communities of people who share common worldviews, practices, and ways of living.

You could think of religion as a story system. Each religious tradition offers stories about how to understand life, what is right or wrong, and what might exist beyond our world. All religions began with stories told by one generation to the next. Some of these stories were eventually written down. They became sacred texts. Religious traditions turn to these texts for guidance and ritual practice.

The Role of Religion

While religions are often shaped by ancient stories, they are not unaffected by the passage of time. Religions evolve in both big and small ways. The term *religion* has come to mean different things to different people. Even members of the same religious community have different ways of thinking about and engaging with their spiritual tradition. Religious beliefs can vary greatly. But there are a few things all religions tend to have in common.

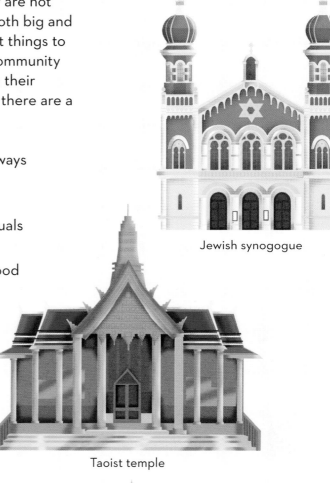

Jewish synogogue

Rituals and practices: These are the styles of worship, ways of eating, and other actions that help express beliefs.

Sacred places and objects: These have significance because of their roles in the religion's history or in its rituals and practices.

Ethics: These are views about what is right or wrong, good or bad, moral or immoral behavior.

Role models: These figures are raised up as powerful examples of how to live the teachings of the religion.

Finally, and perhaps most significantly, religions give people a sense of **meaning and purpose**. That's no small task!

Taoist temple

Christian church

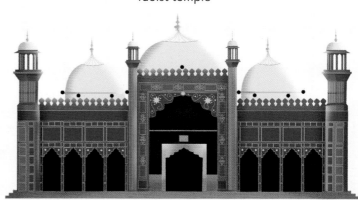

Muslim mosque

The Big Questions

People often seek meaning and purpose by asking big questions about human existence—questions like these:

• Who created us and the world around us?

• Why are we here?

• How should we live? How should we treat one another?

• Why is there suffering and evil in the world?

• What happens to us when we die?

Religions seek to answer these big, big questions. For many people, having answers to these questions brings great comfort.

Theism

To help answer the big, big questions, many religions look beyond the natural world and its inhabitants. They embrace *theism*, the belief in the existence of a God or gods. Different religions have adopted different forms of theism.

Some religions are **monotheistic**. People who practice these religions believe there is one God who created and sustains the universe. Other religions are **polytheistic**. Their followers believe in multiple gods and goddesses. **Henotheistic** religions involve the belief that there are many gods and goddesses but that they all come from the same divine source or power. **Pantheism** is the belief that the divine and the natural world are one and the same—that is, God *is* the natural world. **Transtheistic** traditions may or may not acknowledge divine existence, but in either case, it is not central to the religion.

Why Does It Matter?

Religion has shaped world history. It has been a source of conflict and violence as well as a source of inspiration for art, music, and literature. Religion has guided activists fighting for social justice and human rights. And while religion is often practiced in private and personal ways, it influences how people engage with their greater community.

The vast majority of people in the world hold religious beliefs of some kind. No matter where you fall among the many world religions, it's important to stay curious about what others believe.

HINDUISM

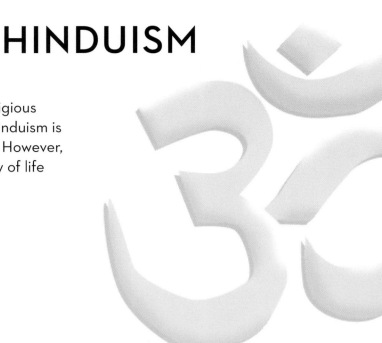

Hinduism encompasses a range of religious ideas, beliefs, and practices. Today, Hinduism is the third-largest religion in the world. However, many Hindus consider Hinduism a way of life rather than a religion.

. . . .

History

Hinduism has no single founder or single sacred text. This makes it difficult to trace the religion to a specific origin. But many scholars agree it is the world's oldest religion. Parts of Hinduism date back more than three thousand years!

The Indus River Valley is an important place in Hinduism's long history. This region covers what is now Pakistan and northwest India. It was home to the Indus Valley Civilization. In 1500 BCE, this ancient civilization encountered Aryan migrants from central Asia. From this encounter emerged the first writings containing some of the central beliefs of Hinduism. The practices of Hinduism eventually spread from this valley across the entire Indian subcontinent.

Today, most Hindus live in India. Hinduism also has a strong presence in nearby Nepal, Bangladesh, Sri Lanka, and Malaysia. There are large Hindu populations outside of Asia, including the United States, the United Kingdom, and South Africa.

Timeline of Important Dates

1500 BCE

. . . .

The Indus Valley Civilization encounters Aryan migrants. These groups produce the first writings to contain core Hindu beliefs.

1500–1200 BCE

The Vedas, originally a set of hymns (songs of praise), are written down. They become a collection of Hindu sacred writings.

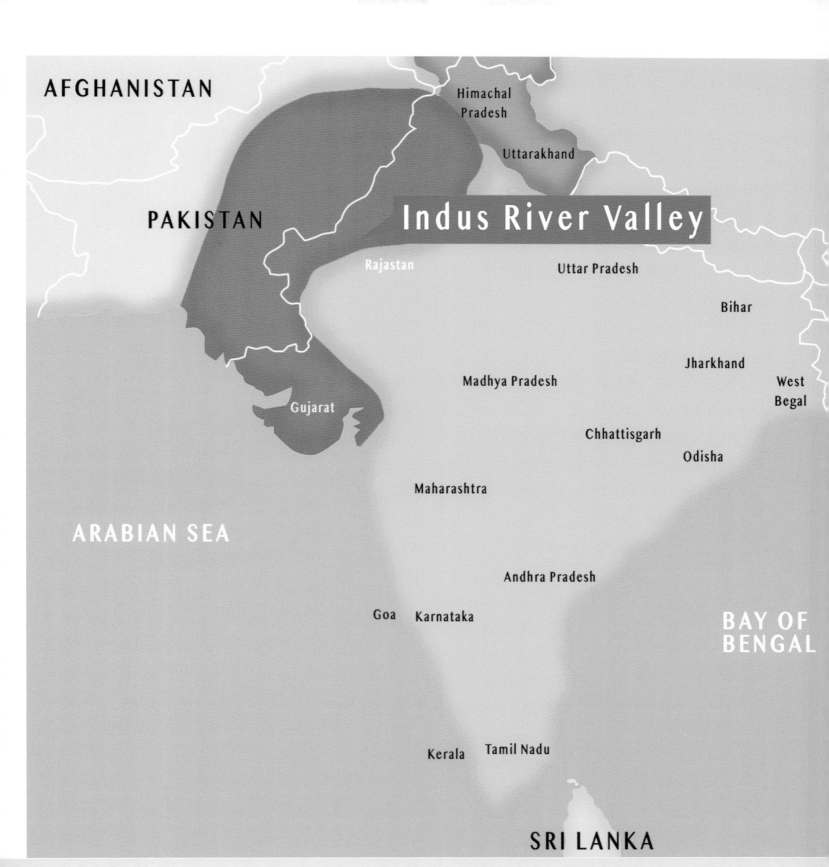

AFGHANISTAN

PAKISTAN

Himachal
Pradesh

Uttarakhand

Indus River Valley

Rajastan

Uttar Pradesh

Bihar

Jharkhand

West
Begal

Madhya Pradesh

Chhattisgarh

Odisha

Gujarat

Maharashtra

ARABIAN SEA

Andhra Pradesh

Goa   Karnataka

BAY OF
BENGAL

Kerala   Tamil Nadu

SRI LANKA

800-500 BCE	500-100 BCE	400 BCE-400 CE
The Upanishads, a series of philosophical commentaries on the Vedas, are created.	The Ramayana, a beloved epic poem containing Hindu teachings about appropriate conduct, is written.	The Mahabharata, another epic poem about Hindu history and moral law, is composed.

Gods and Goddesses

Hinduism embraces beliefs that honor many gods and goddesses. For this reason, it is sometimes referred to as a polytheistic religion. However, many Hindus believe these gods and goddesses come from a single divine source, called Brahman. In this sense, Hinduism can be considered henotheistic.

In Hinduism, the divine source, Brahman, is believed by many to have three main forms. They are Brahma, Vishnu, and Shiva.

FUN FACT

Hindus believe that each person possesses an eternal soul-self called an *atman*. According to the Upanishads, the atman is part of the divine source, Brahman.

Brahma: the creator. Brahma is believed to have created the universe and all beings.

Vishnu: the preserver or sustainer of life. Vishnu is responsible for restoring peace and order.

Shiva: the destroyer or recycler. Shiva is responsible for destruction and death, which gives way to rebirth and new life.

Karma, Dharma, and Moksha

A key concept in the Hindu tradition is reincarnation. This is the idea that life is a constant cycle of death and rebirth. Those who believe in reincarnation believe that after a person dies, they are reborn into a new life. Hindus call this cycle *samsara*, or a state of wandering.

The new life into which one is reborn is based on *karma*, the universal law of cause and effect. Karma states that we all face the consequences of our actions and inaction. What we do in our current life will lead to suffering or rewards in our next lives.

For Hindus, the key to living a good life and reaping rewards in the next is *dharma*. Dharma is an individualized code of good conduct and moral duty. Karma falls in the favor of those who follow dharma. And it's through good karma that one is eventually freed from the cycle of reincarnation. When this happens, one is said to reach ultimate spiritual fulfillment, or *moksha*.

Other Notable Hindu Deities

Lakshmi: the goddess of wealth and good fortune

Ganesha: the lord of beginnings and remover of obstacles

Devi: the Great Goddess or Mother Goddess. All goddesses are manifestations of Devi. These include Lakshmi and Saraswati.

Saraswati: the goddess of learning and knowledge

Krishna: a playful god and an incarnation (a human form) of Vishnu

Hindu Castes

For thousands of years, a social hierarchy has divided Hindus into four main classes, or castes, based on their karma.

- **Brahmins:** the intellectual and spiritual leaders
- **Kshatriyas:** the protectors and public servants
- **Vaisyas:** the skillful producers
- **Shudras:** the unskilled laborers

A fifth group, **Dalits**, belong to no caste and are therefore at the bottom of society.

> **FUN FACT**
>
> Today, India reserves a portion of university seats and government jobs for people from traditionally underrepresented communities. There have even been Dalit presidents of India!

For centuries, caste practices influenced many aspects of religious and social life in India. For example, upper and lower castes did not live in the same communities, and people did not marry outside their caste. The Hindu caste system still exists today. However, there are more opportunities for individuals in lower castes to get an education and hold influential positions. Marriage between people of different castes is also more accepted than it used to be.

EXPLORE MORE

Hindu temples can be found in many communities in the United States where Indian Americans live. Many of these temples offer tours to the public. You can also find virtual tours online.

Puja

For Hindus, worship is called *puja*. It can take place at a temple, where Hindus go to encounter the divine in an experience called *darshan*. But puja also takes place at home. Many Hindu households have a shrine (a space for worship) dedicated to a particular god or goddess. Puja usually involves making an offering to a statue or image of the deity. Common offerings include flowers, fruit, and water.

Yoga

Yoga, an exercise that incorporates breathing and meditation (thinking quietly), originates in Hinduism. Traditional yoga includes a wide range of physical and spiritual practices designed to unite one with the divine. Yoga has also become a popular practice among non-Hindus to promote physical and mental wellness.

My Faith in My Words

"I wake up at sunrise and do yoga with my dad and sister."

Ved, age 10

King Cobra Pose

Cow Pose

Tree Pose

Easy Pose

Triangle Pose

FUN FACT

Tulsi Gabbard of Hawaii was the first Hindu elected to the US Congress in 2013. She took the oath of office on the Bhagavad Gita.

Sacred Texts

Hindus look to a number of writings as sacred texts that inform their beliefs and practices. Practices that involve sacred texts include chanting, reciting, and memorizing portions of them.

The Vedas: the oldest Hindu sacred texts, composed around 1500 BCE. The Vedas are a collection of hymns, prayers, instructions for rituals, and other religious writings.

The Upanishads: the concluding sections of the Vedas. These writings take the form of dialogues between teachers and students that comment on the wisdom of the Vedas.

The Ramayana: an epic poem that tells the story of Rama, the god of righteousness and virtue. In the poem, Rama rescues his wife from a demon-king.

EXPLORE MORE

There are many kid-friendly versions of the Ramayana. Check one out at your local library!

The Mahabharata: an epic poem that contains the Bhagavad Gita, or "Song of God." The well-loved Bhagavad Gita follows the god Krishna and the warrior Arjuna as they discuss duty, action, knowledge, and devotion.

Holidays

In India, Hindu deities are honored throughout the year with local festivals. But some holidays are celebrated by Hindus across India and the world. Two of the most celebrated Hindu holidays are Diwali and Holi.

Diwali is a five-day festival that usually takes place between October and November. For many Hindus, this holiday celebrates the triumph of good over evil. Hindus honor various deities during Diwali, including Rama and Krishna. The festival is marked by feasts, fireworks, and the lighting of clay lamps.

Holi is a festival marking the beginning of spring. It usually takes place in March. Like Diwali, Holi signifies the victory of good over evil. For many, it celebrates the love between the god Krishna and the goddess Radha. During Holi, people throw brightly colored powder into the air and at one another. Holi has become known and celebrated around the world as the Festival of Colors.

Food

Hindu scriptures encourage compassion and nonviolence toward all living things. For this reason, many Hindus choose to eat a diet free of meat. Many who do eat meat avoid beef. This is because, to many Hindus, the cow is considered a sacred symbol of life.

Hinduism in Action

The most recognized Hindu figure is **Mohandas Gandhi**, who lived from 1869 to 1948. Gandhi combined his Hindu beliefs with teachings from Christian scripture. These beliefs influenced Gandhi's activism. He created and led a nonviolent movement for Indian independence from Britain.

Sewa International is an organization based on the Hindu belief in selfless service to all humanity. The organization provides humanitarian aid and disaster relief in the United States and seventeen countries throughout the world.

My Faith in My Words

"My favorite holiday is Holi because of all the colors, sweets, and festivity. It represents good over evil."

Ved, age 10

AFGHANISTAN

BUDDHISM

Buddhism is a religion based on the teachings of the Buddha, Siddhartha Gautama, a spiritual leader who lived and taught in India about 2,500 years ago. Followers of Buddhism often refer to the spiritual tradition as the *dharma*, or teachings. Today, Buddhists make up about 7 percent of the world's population.

PAKISTAN

My Faith in My Words

"[Buddha] chose to solve the suffering in the world when he didn't have to; he could have stayed in his palace."

Anna, age 15

Timeline of Important Dates

Around 560 BCE

Siddhartha Gautama is born in present-day Nepal.

Around 525 BCE

Gautama achieves enlightenment through meditation and becomes known as the Buddha.

Around 480 BCE

The Buddha dies in India at about eighty years old.

History

The founder of Buddhism was born Siddhartha Gautama around 560 BCE in what is now the country of Nepal. Gautama grew up as a prince in the palace of his wealthy family. But when he discovered all the suffering that took place beyond his palace walls, Gautama left his life of comfort.

Gautama spent several years seeking truth and meaning. He became skilled in meditation. It is through meditation that Gautama is believed to have found enlightenment, an awakening to inner peace, wisdom, and compassion.

Gautama spent the rest of his life traveling through India, sharing his wisdom and teaching others how to achieve enlightenment. He gained followers and became known as the *Buddha*, which means "awakened." Buddhist philosophy spread from India to East and Southeast Asia. Today, large populations of Buddhists are found in China, Thailand, Japan, and Myanmar.

CHINA

NEPAL   **BHUTAN**

INDIA   **BANGLADESH**

MYANMAR

200 BCE–200 CE	Around 30 BCE	700s CE
The Mahayana Sutras are written. These texts discuss concepts central to Mahayana Buddhism.	The Pali Canon is completed. This is the earliest written record of the Buddha's teachings.	The Tibetan Book of the Dead is written. This text details the stages between death and rebirth according to the Tibetan Buddhist tradition.

The Eightfold Path

The Buddha taught that the path to end suffering has eight parts and involves wisdom, ethical conduct, and meditation.

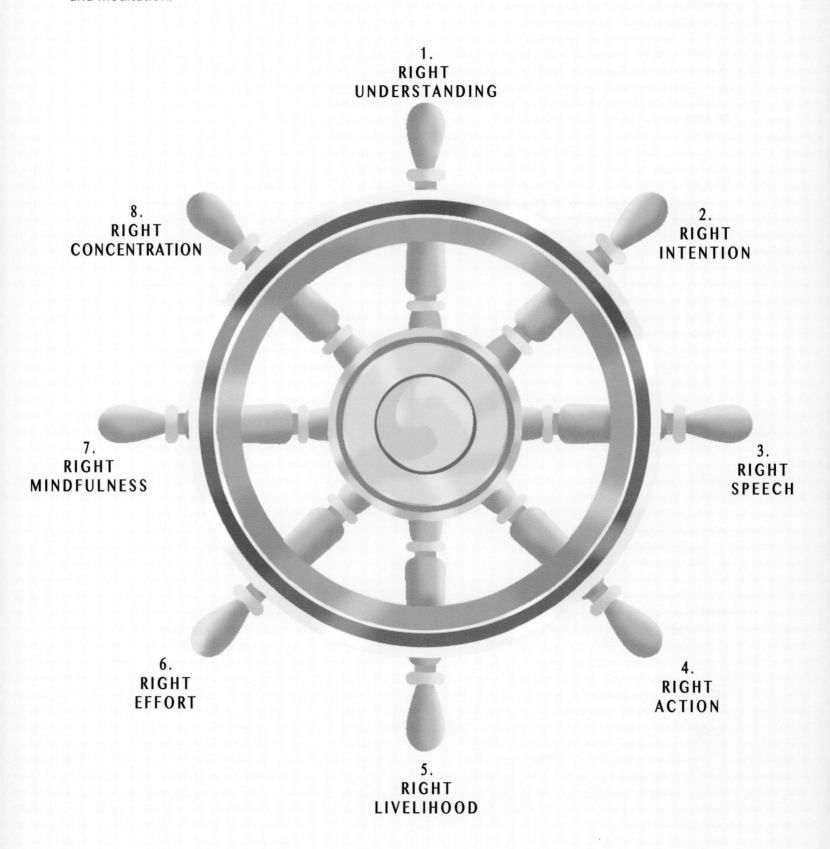

The Four Noble Truths

The Buddha's teachings were based on ideas known as the Four Noble Truths. These truths relate to the cause and end of suffering.

1. **Suffering (*dukkha*):** Being alive means suffering. Humans suffer from illness and death. We also suffer from feeling unsatisfied or unfulfilled.

2. **The cause of suffering (*samudaya*):** The root of all suffering lies in misplaced desire. This is desire that comes from greed, ignorance, or hatred.

3. **The end of suffering (*nirhodha*):** There is a cure to suffering, and it lies in freeing oneself from misplaced desires.

4. **The path to the end of suffering (*magga*):** One can reach the end of suffering by following the Eightfold Path.

Nirvana

According to the Buddha, the Eightfold Path is the way to enlightenment. When one achieves enlightenment, one is said to reach *nirvana*. Nirvana is a state of spiritual joy and compassion, free of fear or other negative emotions.

Some Buddhists believe that until one reaches nirvana, one suffers a continuous cycle of death and rebirth. Through enlightenment, one is freed from this cycle.

Theravada and Mahayana Buddhism

There are two main types of Buddhism: Theravada and Mahayana. A key difference between the two groups relates to the idea of nirvana. Theravada Buddhists strive to achieve enlightenment and reach nirvana through strict practices. Mahayana Buddhists, on the other hand, emphasize helping others achieve enlightenment in addition to themselves. This means staying in the cycle of death and rebirth so that others may reach nirvana. Individuals dedicated to this role are known as bodhisattvas.

Buddhism and Theism

Some Buddhists believe in divine beings. However, the Buddhist tradition does not worship a supreme god or deity. For this reason, some consider Buddhism to neither acknowledge nor deny the existence of a God or gods.

Sacred texts

In Buddhism, sacred texts are called *sutras*, or threads.

The **Pali Canon** is the earliest collection of the Buddha's teachings. It is also known as the Tipitaka, or "Three Baskets," because it contains three parts.

The **Mahayana Sutras** is a collection of more than two thousand sutras. They discuss bodhisattvas and other concepts embraced by Mahayana Buddhists.

The **Tibetan Book of the Dead** is a Tibetan Buddhist text. It describes the stages an individual goes though between death and rebirth. This text is usually recited in the presence of a recently deceased person.

FUN FACT

Tibetan Buddhists believe the phase between death and rebirth lasts forty-nine days. The Tibetan Book of the Dead is meant to guide the dead through this phase.

Karma

Buddhism embraces *karma*, the universal law of cause and effect. This law dictates that one's actions will affect one's experience today as well as the state in which one is later reborn. Karma encourages Buddhists to live a good life through good behavior.

My Faith in My Words

"[Mindfulness] comes down to being present in the moment. One of the ideas I think about is the idea of a glass being half empty or half full. According to Buddhism, both are wrong—the glass just is."

Anna, age 15

Rituals

Buddhists perform a number of rituals to show their devotion to the Buddha and his teachings. These rituals include puja, meditation, and chanting.

Puja is a form of ceremony that involves leaving gifts, or offerings. Buddhists carry out puja at home or in a temple. They offer flowers, candles, or other gifts to show respect and reverence for the Buddha.

Meditation is central to Buddhist practice. Buddhists meditate to increase their mindfulness and concentration. They believe this mental development brings one closer to enlightenment, just as it did for Gautama. Meditation can take place while sitting, lying down, standing, or walking.

Chanting is a widespread ritual that is often part of meditation. Chanting involves repeating phrases from sacred texts. Buddhists also chant sacred words called mantras.

Five Precepts

Many Buddhists live by a code of ethics known as the Five Precepts. These moral principles call on individuals to abstain from (to choose not to do) the following:

1.
Taking a life

2.
Taking what is not given

3.
Sexual misconduct

4.
False speech, or lying

5.
Using drugs or alcohol

FUN FACT

Some Buddhists hold a string of beads called a *mala* when they chant or meditate. Malas help meditators keep track of their mantra repetitions.

EXPLORE MORE

You can start your own mindfulness meditation practice at home. Take three to five minutes each day to sit quietly, close your eyes, and focus on your breathing. You can also practice mindfulness at mealtime. Try eating slowly, thinking of where your food came from and who helped bring it to your table.

Wesak

Buddhists observe various festivals throughout the year. The most widely celebrated is Wesak. This is a celebration of the Buddha's birth, enlightenment, and death.

Also known as Buddha Day, Wesak takes place in the spring. Buddhists celebrate with lights, candles, and lanterns. Some people release paper lanterns into the sky to symbolize the path to enlightenment.

Monasteries

Monasteries have long been central to the Buddhist tradition. The men and women who live in monasteries are called monks and nuns. These individuals follow strict codes of conduct. They live without material possessions and comforts. They rely on laypeople (people who have not taken religious vows) to donate food and other necessities. Monastics spend much of their time engaging in ritual practices and meditation. Monasteries also hold ceremonies and guided meditations for laypeople to attend.

Buddhism in Action

Thich Nhat Hanh was a Vietnamese Buddhist monk and global spiritual leader. During the Vietnam War in the 1960s, Thich Nhat Hanh and other monks and nuns had a decision to make: Should they continue their monastic way of life or go out and help those suffering from the war? In doing both, Thich Nhat Hanh pioneered the Engaged Buddhism movement. Engaged Buddhists call upon the teachings of the Buddha to inform their actions in dealing with contemporary issues.

In 1982, Thich Nhat Hanh established a monastic community in southwest France. Now known as Plum Village, the community has become the West's largest Buddhist monastery. Based out of Plum Village is the **Earth Holder Community**. This initiative applies Engaged Buddhism to promote racial, social, and environmental justice.

FUN FACT

Tibetan Buddhist monks create detailed patterns called *mandalas* out of colored sand. These patterns take several days to construct. When a mandala is complete, the monks sweep up the sand and pour it into flowing water. The destruction of the mandala is a reminder of the impermanence of all things.

JUDAISM

Judaism is the world's oldest monotheistic religion. It is also the first of what are known as the Abrahamic faiths. The other two are Christianity and Islam. These traditions trace their origins back to the figure Abraham. It is believed that Abraham was the first to believe in the singular God, that is the creator of the universe. Today, most Jews live in the United States and Israel. However, Jewish communities can be found around the world.

Judaism is both a religion and a people. Many Jews consider their faith to be central to their Jewish identity. But many others base their Jewish identity on their heritage or culture. Nonreligious Jews are still considered part of the Jewish people, even if they do not believe in God.

History

Abraham is considered the first ancestor of the Jewish people. He is thought to have lived around 1800 BCE. Jews believe Abraham was the first to form a covenant (a serious agreement or promise) with God.

Abraham's wife, Sarah, their son Isaac, and their grandson Jacob are also central figures in Jewish history. Jacob was later called Israel. His descendants were called Israelites. Over centuries, they became the biblical nation of Israel.

Jewish scripture teaches that Israelites were enslaved in Egypt. In the 1200s BCE, they were led to freedom by Moses, an Israelite who had been adopted by the daughter of the pharaoh (the Egyptian king) when he was a child. As an adult, Moses rejoined his people to lead them out of slavery. It is believed that God worked through Moses to help the Israelites (also known as Hebrews) escape the Egyptian army.

According to the *Torah*, a part of the Hebrew Scriptures, God later renewed the divine covenant with Abraham. But this time, the covenant was formed with the entire Israelite people. Moses received from God a set of rules the Israelites should live by. The best-known of these rules are called the Ten Commandments. Most scholars consider this new covenant to mark the beginning of Judaism. After wandering in the desert for forty years, the Israelites began to live in the region that came to be known as the land of Israel and Judah.

Timeline of Important Dates

1200s BCE	Around 1000 BCE	586 BCE	Around 515 BCE
Moses leads the Israelites to freedom from enslavement in Egypt.	King David rules the Jewish people and his son Solomon builds the first holy temple in Jerusalem.	Solomon's temple is destroyed by the Babylonians.	A second holy temple is built in Jerusalem.

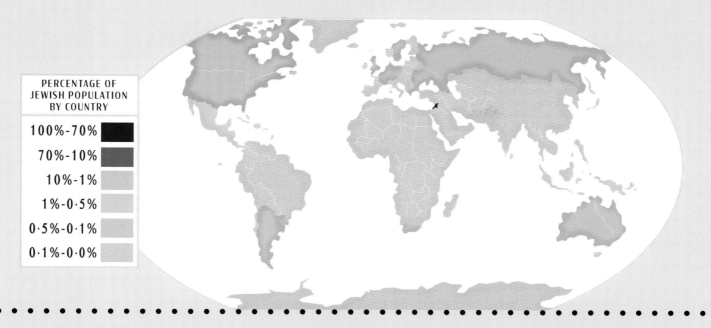

PERCENTAGE OF
JEWISH POPULATION
BY COUNTRY

100%-70%
70%-10%
10%-1%
1%-0·5%
0·5%-0·1%
0·1%-0·0%

Around 1000 BCE, the Israelite people were ruled by King David. King David's son Solomon oversaw the construction of the first temple in Jerusalem. The temple became the center of Judaism, where the people gathered and offered sacrifices to God. After the first temple was destroyed by Babylonian invaders, a second was built around 515 BCE. After Roman forces destroyed the Second Temple in 70 CE, the Jews were driven from their homeland, and they settled throughout Europe and the Middle East.

Jews in Europe lived in segregated towns and neighborhoods. They often faced anti-Semitism (discrimination because they were Jews). Beginning in the 1800s, many European Jews immigrated to the United States due to hardship and persecution. The most devastating persecution of Jews was the **Holocaust**. This was the mass murder of millions of Jews and other groups by German Nazis between 1933 and 1945.

Around the time of the Holocaust, many Jews returned to their homeland in the Middle East. Many wanted to create a Jewish state. In 1948, world leaders established the State of Israel in the region of Palestine, home to many Palestinians of the Christian and Muslim faiths. This led to decades of conflict, which continues today, between Israelis and Palestinians.

EXPLORE MORE

Read *The Diary of a Young Girl* by Anne Frank. The book follows the experience of its teenage author, a Jewish girl whose family hid for two years in a small set of rooms in an old office building during the Holocaust. She was discovered and died in the Bergen-Belsen concentration camp in 1945.

70 CE

The Romans destroy the Second Temple and Jews are driven from their homeland.

1933–1945 CE

Six million Jews and millions of others are murdered by German Nazis and their allies during the Holocaust.

1948 CE

World leaders establish the State of Israel in part of the region known as Palestine.

Ethical Monotheism

Judaism teaches ethical monotheism. This is the belief in one God who has given humanity moral principles to live by. Jews believe their purpose in this world is to engage in *tikkun olam*, a Hebrew phrase meaning "repair of the world." They fulfill this calling through acts of charity and justice.

Judaism the religion is based on a belief that God is both present in all of creation and transcendent, or beyond all earthly things. Some Jews believe in an all-knowing, all-powerful God who rewards the good and punishes the evil.

Movements

There are many branches, or movements, of Jewish religious life. The three listed here are the largest branches of modern Judaism in North America. They differ in their understanding of how to follow Jewish law.

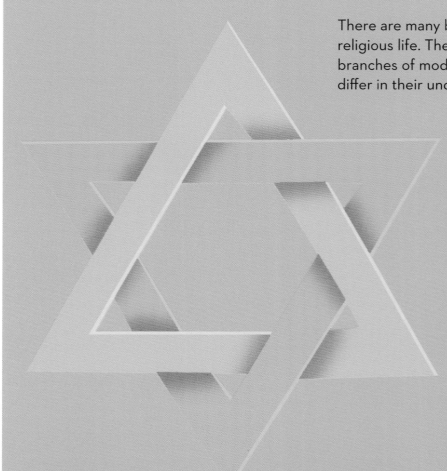

Orthodox Judaism upholds strict observance of traditional laws and rituals. For example, most Orthodox Jews refrain from working or driving on Shabbat, or the sabbath—the Jewish day of rest.

Conservative Judaism honors traditional laws but teaches that they should be adapted to modern times.

Reform Judaism leaves observance of Jewish law up to individual choice. The movement emphasizes ethical traditions, social justice, and inclusivity.

Sacred Texts

The Hebrew Scriptures, also known as the Tanakh, is the sacred text of Judaism. Much of Jewish history is contained in this text. The Tanakh consists of three parts: the Torah, the Nevi'im, and the Ketuvim.

The Torah, or Law, is also known as the Five Books of Moses, or the Pentateuch. It holds the Jewish law as it was revealed by God to Moses. Jews consider the Torah a book of teachings or instructions to live by.

The Nevi'im, known in English as the Prophets, consists of eight books. These books contain the words of various prophets.

The Ketuvim, or Writings, is a collection of assorted writings, including poetry, stories, history, and wisdom.

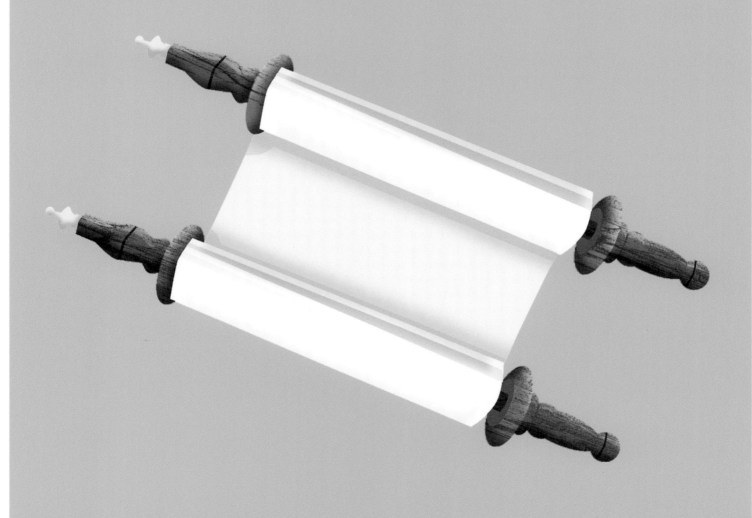

As scholars discussed how to interpret the Tanakh, they composed the Talmud. This text was written over centuries and in several locations. It contains the Mishnah and the Gemara. The Mishnah is a collection of oral teachings of Jewish law. The Gemara contains commentaries on these oral laws. It includes the interpretations of thousands of rabbis, or Jewish religious leaders.

Synagogue

The Jewish place of worship is called the *synagogue*. Jews gather here for daily or weekly prayer services depending on their personal practices. Jewish holidays and special rituals also bring people to communal worship and celebrations. Synagogue services are often led by a rabbi and a cantor, or musical leader.

Inside the synagogue, many Jewish men wear a head covering called a *kippah* to show respect for God. Women might wear a kippah, but some choose to wear a headscarf, a hat, or no head covering.

Shabbat

Shabbat is a day of rest and prayer in Judaism. On this day, Jews adhere to the fourth of the Ten Commandments, "Remember the sabbath day, and keep it holy."

Shabbat begins on Friday at sunset and ends at sundown on Saturday. Many Jewish families try to avoid shopping, chores, and cooking during this time, as was the custom in biblical times. Many attend prayer services at synagogues. Jews may also observe Shabbat by going on walks, taking naps, and gathering for family meals. On Friday evenings, it is tradition to light candles, drink wine, and eat *challah*, a soft, egg-rich bread.

My Faith in My Words

"I really enjoy Shabbat. It's nice to say the prayers over the candles, wine, and challah and to spend time at dinner with my family. It's something to look forward to each week."

Soren, age 12

FUN FACT

The traditional Hebrew greeting on Shabbat is "Shabbat shalom." In Hebrew, shalom means "peace." Some say the Yiddish equivalent, "Gut Shabbes!"

FUN FACT

About 22 percent of American Jews eat a strictly kosher diet.

Kashrut

One of the many commandments in the Torah is for Jews to eat food that is kosher. This is food that is permitted by and prepared according to *kashrut*, or Jewish dietary law. Kashrut, for example, forbids eating pork, shellfish, and predatory animals. It also specifies a proper way for animals to be slaughtered if they will be eaten. Many Jews follow some but not all of the dietary laws. Orthodox Jews observe kashrut in its entirety.

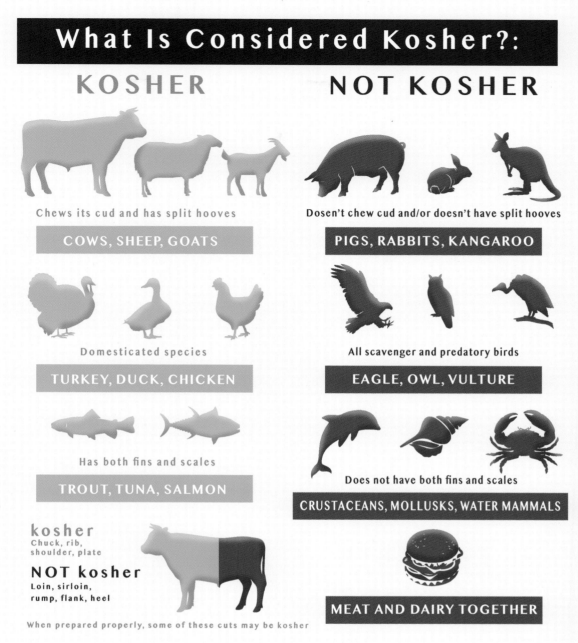

What Is Considered Kosher?:

KOSHER

Chews its cud and has split hooves

COWS, SHEEP, GOATS

Domesticated species

TURKEY, DUCK, CHICKEN

Has both fins and scales

TROUT, TUNA, SALMON

kosher
Chuck, rib, shoulder, plate

NOT kosher
Loin, sirloin, rump, flank, heel

When prepared properly, some of these cuts may be kosher

NOT KOSHER

Dosen't chew cud and/or doesn't have split hooves

PIGS, RABBITS, KANGAROO

All scavenger and predatory birds

EAGLE, OWL, VULTURE

Does not have both fins and scales

CRUSTACEANS, MOLLUSKS, WATER MAMMALS

MEAT AND DAIRY TOGETHER

Judaism in Action

Abraham Joshua Heschel was a Jewish rabbi, professor, and activist for peace and civil rights. Heschel was born in 1907 in Warsaw, Poland. In 1940, he immigrated to the United States, where he became a professor at New York's Jewish Theological Seminary of America. During the 1960s, Heschel was deeply involved with the American civil rights movement. He gave speeches on race, religion, war, and injustice. He also marched for voting rights for African Americans alongside Martin Luther King Jr.

American Jewish World Service (AJWS) is a global community of Jewish people committed to ending poverty and promoting human rights. Based in New York City, AJWS supports local organizations in developing countries to provide disaster relief, end human rights violations, defend natural resources, and more. To provide this support, AJWS educates and trains American Jewish leaders to advocate for global justice in government policies and laws.

Holidays

There are many Jewish holidays, some celebratory and some solemn or serious in nature. Two important Jewish holidays are Rosh Hashanah and Yom Kippur.

Rosh Hashanah is the Jewish New Year. It takes place in September or October and commemorates the birth of the world. Jews observe Rosh Hashanah by reflecting on the past year and the deeds they have done. Special services take place at synagogues. At home, Jews eat festive meals that include apples dipped in honey. This treat symbolizes hope for a sweet new year.

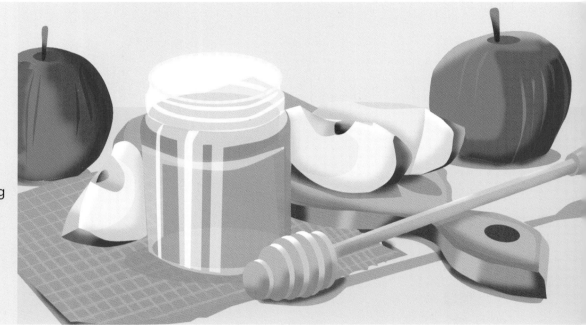

FUN FACT

Rosh Hashanah rituals include the blowing of the shofar, a ram's-horn trumpet, as a call for Jews to repent (acknowledge regret for having done something wrong). Another ritual, Tashlich, is the tossing of pebbles or breadcrumbs into a body of water. This symbolizes casting off the sins of the previous year.

Yom Kippur takes place ten days after Rosh Hashanah. Often called the Day of Atonement, it is a time to make up for misdeeds during the previous year. Many Jews refrain from eating or drinking on this holy day. Jews also attend the synagogue and ask God to forgive their sins. Judaism teaches that Yom Kippur is the day that God seals the fate of each individual for the coming year.

Another notable Jewish holiday is **Passover**, or *Pesach*. It commemorates the Israelites' escape from enslavement in Egypt, known as the Exodus. Passover takes place in March or April and lasts either seven or eight days, depending on the tradition that's followed. Jewish families begin Passover with a ritual meal called the *seder*. During this meal, families tell the story of the Exodus.

EXPLORE MORE

Some synagogues host model seders before Passover to educate those unfamiliar with the ritual.

FUN FACT

Jews eat unleavened bread called *matzah* during the seder meal. The bread is unleavened (made without yeast) to represent the Israelites not having time to let their bread dough rise as they prepared to escape from Egyptian slavery.

Coming of Age

Jewish teens celebrate the passage into adulthood at around thirteen years old. This is when they become responsible for observing Jewish law and fully participating in synagogue services. The coming-of-age ceremony is called a *bat mitzvah* for girls and a *bar mitzvah* for boys. More recently, the gender-neutral term *b'nei mitzvah* has become common. During the ritual, the teen typically reads from the Torah and leads the community in prayer. A celebration with family and friends often follows the ceremony.

Women and men traditionally hold different roles and responsibilities in Judaism. Because of this, not all Jewish communities hold bat mitzvahs. Orthodox Jews hold a *bat chayil*, or "daughter of valor," ceremony for girls.

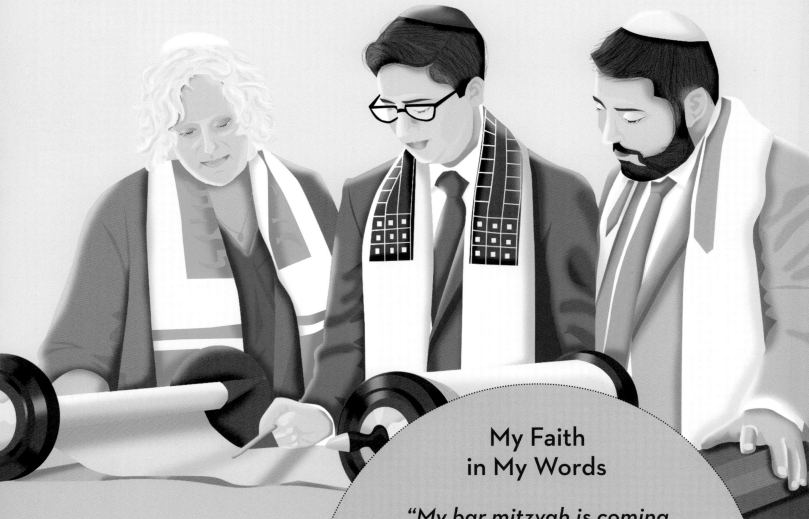

FUN FACT

Bar mitzvah means "son of the commandment" and bat mitzvah means "daughter of the commandment."

My Faith in My Words

"My bar mitzvah is coming up next year, and my Torah portions . . . list the things needed to build the Tabernacle and the skills of the people who made it. I like thinking about these stories because I enjoy making things, and this story is about my ancestors using their skills to make things too."

Soren, age 12

CHRISTIANITY

Like Judaism, Christianity is an Abrahamic faith. It recognizes the God of Abraham.

The Christian faith is based on the life, death, resurrection, and teachings of the religious leader Jesus Christ, whom its followers believe is both fully human and fully divine. Christianity developed as a small group within Judaism. Today, it is the most widely followed religion in the world.

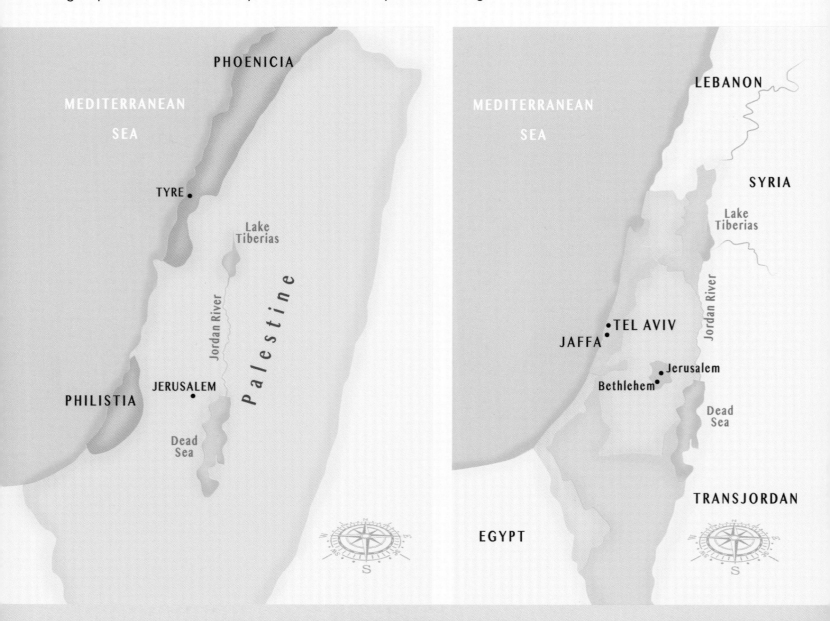

Timeline of Important Dates

1200-100 BCE

The Hebrew scriptures (what Christians often call the Old Testament) are written. This collection of writings makes up the first part of the Bible, the sacred text of Christianity.

Around 4 BCE

Jesus is born in Bethlehem.

Around 27 CE

Jesus begins preaching to the public in the land of Israel.

History

Jesus was born around 4 BCE in Bethlehem, a town in present-day Palestine. He grew up Jewish. At around thirty years old, he began preaching to the public in the land of Israel.

Jesus became known for his teachings. He advocated for compassionate treatment of the poor and outcasts of society, and said he was the Son of God and the Messiah or Christ (both of which mean "anointed one"). He was also said to have performed miracles, such as curing the blind and walking on water. Jesus traveled and taught with men known as the twelve disciples, or apostles.

Around 30 CE, Jesus was arrested by Roman authorities and charged with blasphemy, which means claiming to be God or to speak for God. He was sentenced to death and crucified in Jerusalem.

According to Christian scripture, Jesus's body went missing three days after his death. Christians believe he had been resurrected, or raised from the dead. The resurrected Jesus was said to appear to many of his followers before ascending to heaven.

After Jesus's death, Christianity began as a Jewish sect. Those who converted to Christianity were persecuted by Roman leaders. This changed around 312, when Emperor Constantine of Rome embraced Christianity. After this turning point, Christianity grew and split into three main branches: Catholic, Protestant, and Orthodox.

Today, Christians are found throughout the world. Countries with the largest Christian populations include the United States, Brazil, Mexico, and Russia.

FUN FACT

Jesus is an important figure in Islam's sacred text, the Qur'an. However, Islam regards Jesus as one of many prophets, or people who reveal God's will, while Christianity views Jesus as the Son of God.

Around 30 CE

Jesus is charged with blasphemy and put to death. Three days later, he is resurrected.

50–100 CE

The New Testament is written. This collection of writings makes up the second part of the Christian Bible.

312 CE

Persecution of Christians comes to an end when Emperor Constantine of Rome embraces Christianity.

The Trinity

Christianity is a monotheistic religion. Christians believe there is one God. They also believe that Jesus is the Son of God.

The Christian God is said to be one God in three parts, known as the Trinity. As **Creator**, God is the creator and judge of the world. As **Savior**, God came as Jesus Christ to offer forgiveness for sins and a new way of relating to God. As **Holy Spirit**, God is the life-giving presence in the world and guides, comforts, and encourages Christians.

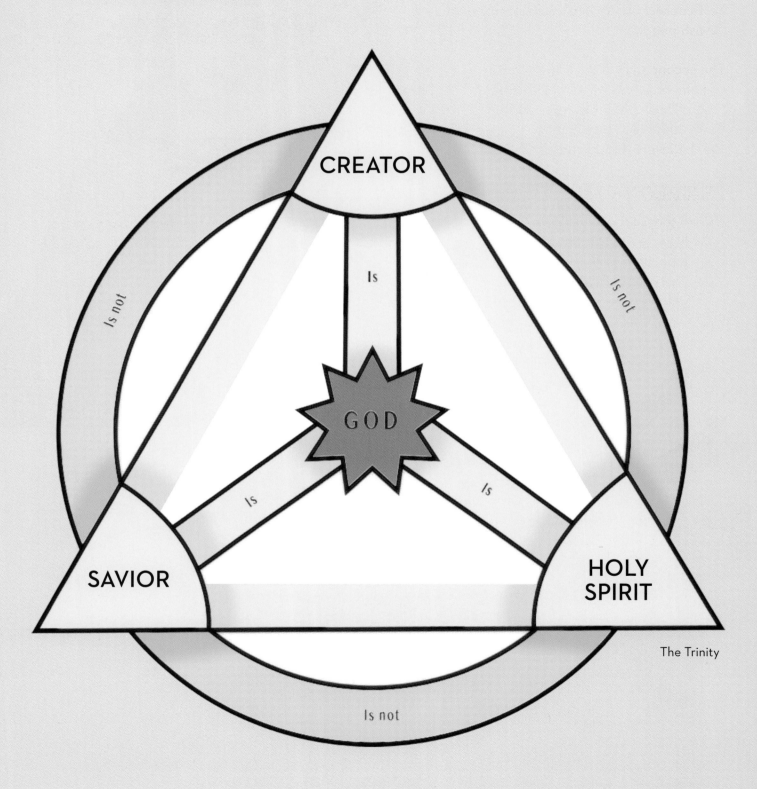

The Trinity

The Bible

The sacred text of Christianity is called the Bible. The first part of the Bible is the Hebrew Scriptures, or Old Testament. These writings were composed during the period between 1200 and 100 BCE and describe the history of the Jewish people, Jewish laws, and the stories of different prophets, including Moses. The Old Testament is about God's relationship with the Jewish people.

The second part of the Christian Bible is the New Testament. It was written by Christians after Jesus's death. The New Testament describes the life, teachings, death, and resurrection of Jesus. It is about God's relationship with believers through Jesus Christ.

EXPLORE MORE

Read the Gospel of Mark in the New Testament. It reads like a documentary, narrating the life of Jesus from one scene to the next.

FUN FACT

The Christian and Jewish faiths both hold the Hebrew Scriptures, or Old Testament, as a sacred text. However, only Christians embrace the New Testament. Christians believe the Old Testament tells of the coming of a savior, and they believe Jesus fulfilled this prophecy.

The Afterlife

Christians believe in life after death. This belief is based on the story of the resurrection of Jesus Christ. Christians refer to this afterlife as heaven, or eternal life.

Churches

Christians belong to worship communities called *churches*. Members of a church gather for worship services led by a church leader. Many Christians attend church services each week on Sunday, which is considered a holy day. Church services often include hymns (songs of praise), readings from the Bible, prayer, and a sermon (a speech giving religious instruction by a priest or minister). In many churches, a central part of the service is the Eucharist.

The Eucharist

The Eucharist is a meal within the church service. In this ritual, Christians have bread and wine or grape juice. The meal commemorates the Last Supper, Jesus's final meal with his disciples. Christians believe Christ meets them in the bread and wine/juice. Some churches consider the bread and wine/juice to be symbols of the body and blood of Christ. Other churches believe the bread and wine become the actual body and blood of Christ.

FUN FACT

Eucharist is a Greek term for "thanksgiving." Churches may also refer to the Eucharist as Holy Communion or the Lord's Supper.

Baptism

Individuals are admitted into the Christian church through baptism. In this ritual, a religious leader pours or sprinkles water on the head of the new member or lowers their whole body into a pool of water. In some churches, parents have their kids baptized during infancy. Other churches reserve baptism for believers only.

Prayer

Christians communicate with God through prayer. Christians pray together at church. They also pray on their own, whenever they are moved to do so. Many Christians address God or Jesus during prayer. Some also direct their prayers to holy figures called *saints* or to Mary, the mother of Jesus. Christians ask these figures to appeal to God on their behalf.

Values

Christians try to live by Jesus's teachings. Jesus called on his followers to do the following:

- Love God above all else
- Love others as you love yourself
- Love your enemies
- Do not judge others
- Forgive others
- Seek forgiveness for your sins
- Care for the poor and others in need

My Faith in My Words

"To me, being part of my religious tradition . . . means helping others in need. I like helping others no matter what."

Anya, age 11

Holidays

The two most important Christian holidays are Christmas and Easter. Christians also observe a number of holy days leading up to and following these main holidays.

Christmas is a celebration of the birth of Jesus Christ. Christians celebrate Christmas by giving gifts, attending church services, and retelling the story of Jesus's birth. For many, Christmas takes place on December 25. Orthodox Christians observe the holiday on January 6. This holy day is called Epiphany. It marks the day when Jesus was revealed to the world.

My Faith in My Words

"Christmas is a time of hope, joy, and happiness."

Anya, age 11

FUN FACT

The most common telling of Jesus's birth says he was born among animals in a stable and laid in a manger. Popular images depict newborn Jesus surrounded by his mother, Mary; his father, Joseph; shepherds and their sheep; and three men known as the three kings, magi, or wise men.

Easter is a celebration of the resurrection of Jesus Christ. Leading up to Easter is Lent, a season of fasting and reflection lasting forty days. On Easter, Christians attend special church services and gather for family meals.

Christianity in Action

Dorothy Day was an American journalist and social activist born in 1897. In the 1920s, Day became a member of the Catholic Church. She cofounded a monthly newspaper called the *Catholic Worker* in the 1930s. Day led a movement advocating for peace and aiding the poor and homeless. She became known as one of the great Catholic lay leaders of the twentieth century.

Bread for the World is a Christian organization founded in 1974. Its goal is to end hunger globally by 2030. By working with churches, college campuses, and nonprofits, Bread for the World urges government officials to address the root causes of hunger.

ISLAM

Islam is a religious tradition whose followers, called Muslims, make up one-fifth of the world's population. Islam is one of the Abrahamic faiths along with Judaism and Christianity. Muslims believe that Abraham was the first prophet to receive messages from God. However, Islam originated with the prophet Muhammad and his followers. Islam is the second-largest and the fastest-growing religion in the world.

FUN FACT

The word *Islam* means "submission to the will of God."

My Faith in My Words

"[The story of prophet Muhammad] teaches patience and how to be humble when people turn their backs on you."

Hafsa, age 12

History

Muslims consider Muhammad to be the final prophet sent by God. Muhammad was born in Mecca, a city in what is now Saudi Arabia, in 570 CE. Around 610, he sought solitude in a mountain cave. There, it is said that he began to receive messages from God through the angel Gabriel. He shared these messages with the people of Mecca.

In 622, Muhammad and his followers fled to the city of Medina to escape persecution. This journey became known as the *Hijrah*, or "migration." It marks the beginning of the Islamic calendar, which is a lunar calendar.

Timeline of Important Dates

570 CE

The prophet Muhammad is born in Mecca, Saudi Arabia.

610 CE

Muhammad receives messages from God while seeking solitude in a cave.

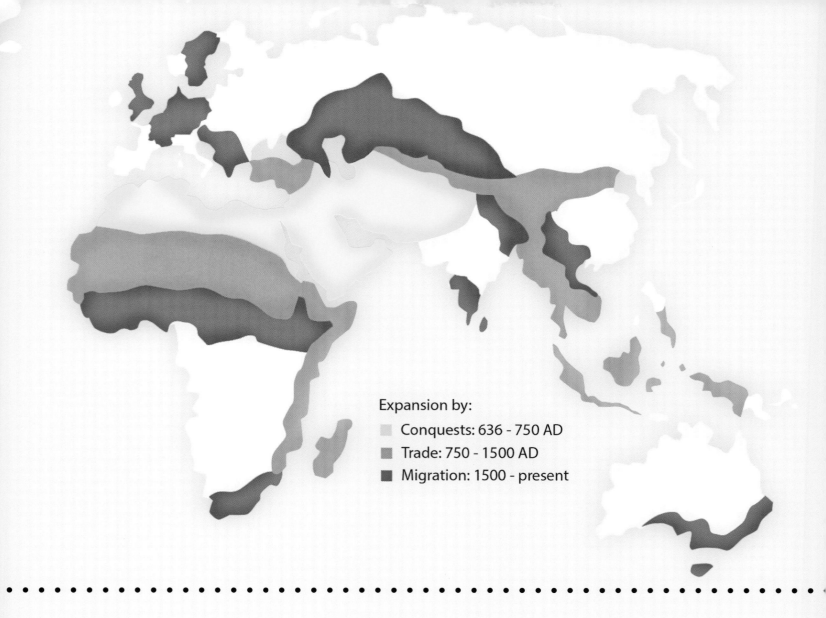

Expansion by:
- Conquests: 636 - 750 AD
- Trade: 750 - 1500 AD
- Migration: 1500 - present

In Medina, Muhammad and his companions formed the first Muslim community. He preached the word of God until his death in 632. After Muhammad's death, a series of leaders, called *caliphs*, succeeded the Prophet. This system of leadership is known as a caliphate.

Through the caliphate, Islam expanded into regions of the Middle East as well as parts of Europe, Africa, and Asia. But the caliphate also divided Muslims. This is because Muslims didn't agree on who should replace Muhammad. This divide led to the two major sects of Islam: the Sunni and the Shia.

Today, the largest Muslim populations are found in South Asia, West Asia, and North Africa.

Sunnis represent roughly 85 percent of Muslims. Most of the other 15 percent identify as Shi'ites.

622 CE

Muhammad and his followers travel to Medina in a journey known as the Hijrah.

632 CE

The death of the prophet Muhammad leads to a series of Muslim leaders called caliphs. Disagreement over rightful caliphs leads to the two major Islamic sects, the Sunni and the Shia.

The Five Pillars

Islam is a monotheistic religion. Muslims believe in and worship one God, called *Allah*, which means "God" in Arabic. One becomes a Muslim by declaring the *Shahadah*: "There is no god but God, and Muhammad is the messenger of God." The Shahadah is the first of what are known as the Five Pillars of Islam.

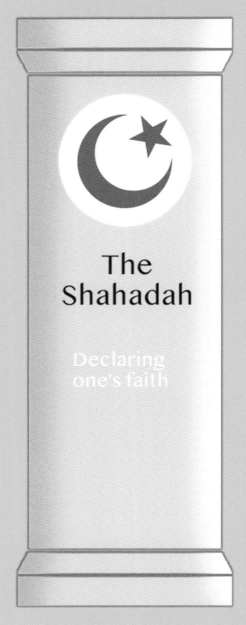

The Shahadah

Declaring one's faith

Salah

Praying five times a day

The Afterlife

Muslims believe in *Akhirah*, or life after death. For those who have performed mostly good deeds, there is *Jannah*, or paradise. This is a place of everlasting bliss. For those who have done more bad than good, there is *Jahannam*, or hell. This is a place of suffering.

Many Muslims believe the afterlife does not begin until the Day of Judgment. This is believed to be a final day in which God judges all of humanity.

Qur'an

The most important holy book of Islam is the Qur'an. Islam teaches that this book contains the messages revealed by God to the prophet Muhammad. Muslims believe the Qur'an is the supreme and final word of God. Muslims read and recite the Qur'an. They believe doing so brings them closer to God.

Hadith

The Hadith is another important text in Islam. It is a collection of the words and teachings of the prophet Muhammad. The Hadith serves as a moral guide to Muslims in their daily life.

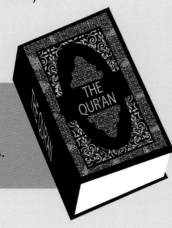

FUN FACT

The Qur'an contains more than 6,000 verses organized into 114 chapters. Many Muslims memorize the full text!

Zakat

Giving to those in need

Sawm

Fasting during Ramadan, the ninth month of the Islamic calendar

Hajj

Making a pilgrimage (a journey to a sacred place) to the holy city of Mecca

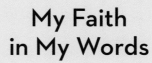

My Faith in My Words

"I have a purpose in life when I wake up each morning knowing I have obligations toward Allah."

Hafsa, age 12

FUN FACT

Ibtihaj Muhammad is an Olympic fencer. In 2016, she was the first American Muslim woman to win an Olympic medal. She was also the first US Olympic athlete to compete wearing a hijab, the traditional head scarf worn by many Muslim women.

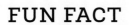

Salah

Muslims are called to pray five times a day. This prayer ritual is called *salah*. It occurs at dawn, midday, late afternoon, sunset, and night. Muslims perform salah at their homes, at places of worship called *mosques*, or wherever they are at the time of prayer.

Before praying, Muslims perform a cleansing ritual called *wudu*. This is a washing of the hands, mouth, nose, face, arms, head, ears, and feet.

Muslims face the holy city of Mecca to pray. They start their prayers by saying *Allahu akbar*, meaning "God is great." Then they do *raka'ah*, a sequence of spoken words and movements that make up a unit of prayer. Salah concludes with the *taslim*. This is the reciting of an Arabic phrase that means "May the peace, mercy, and blessings of God be with you." This phrase is spoken once while facing right and once facing left.

EXPLORE MORE

There are many smartphone apps that guide Muslims in daily prayer. Download and explore one for a day.

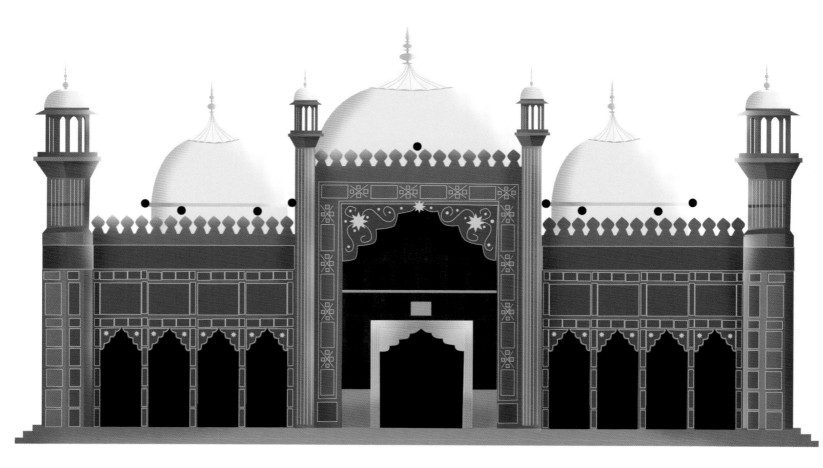

Jumu'ah

For Muslims, Friday is a day of communal worship at a mosque. This Friday prayer is called *Jumu'ah*. It takes the place of the midday prayer. During Jumu'ah, Muslims listen to a sermon (a speech giving religious instruction) by the mosque's worship leader, or *imam*. They also do raka'ah.

Hajj

Muslims must make a pilgrimage to the holy city Mecca at least once in their life if they are able to. This pilgrimage is called *hajj*. Hajj takes place over the course of five days in the twelfth month of the Islamic calendar. More than two million Muslims make this journey every year. Hajj is a symbol of unity among Muslims and of their equality before God.

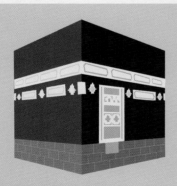

FUN FACT

Muslims perform a number of rituals during hajj. One ritual is to walk seven times around the *Kaaba*, a cube-shaped monument in Mecca. Muslims consider the Kaaba to be the house of God.

Ramadan

Muslims around the world observe Ramadan during the ninth month of the Islamic calendar. Ramadan is a monthlong period of fasting (abstaining from food), prayer, and reflection. During Ramadan, Muslims do not eat or drink from sunrise until sunset. They are urged to read the entire Qur'an during this month.

FUN FACT

The traditional greeting during Ramadan is Ramadan Mubarak, which means "Blessed Month."

Eid al-Fitr

Eid al-Fitr is a major Muslim holiday. Meaning "Festival of Breaking of the Fast," Eid al-Fitr marks the end of Ramadan. The three-day celebration is filled with gatherings of friends and families to feast and exchange gifts. Muslims also take part in communal worship and give zakat during Eid al-Fitr.

FUN FACT

The traditional greeting during Eid al-Fitr and Eid al-Adha is Eid Mubarak, which means "Blessed Feast."

Eid al-Adha

Eid al-Adha is another major holiday in Islam. It means "Festival of the Sacrifice." This holiday commemorates the prophet Abraham's willingness to sacrifice his son for God. Eid al-Adha takes place during the twelfth month of the Islamic calendar. Some Muslims mark the festival by slaughtering an animal. They use the meat to feed family, friends, and community members in need.

Al-Hijrah

Al-Hijrah is the Islamic New Year. It commemorates the journey Muhammad made from Mecca to Medina in 622. Muslims celebrate the new year by making resolutions and spending time with family.

Islam in Action

The **Inner-City Muslim Action Network (IMAN)** was established in 1997 to serve communities of color living in Chicago, Illinois. In 2016, a second branch opened in Atlanta, Georgia. IMAN works from the Muslim tradition to foster health, wellness, and social change in underserved communities.

Muhammad Ali was an American heavyweight boxing champion. Born Cassius Clay, he changed his name in the 1960s when he converted to Islam. In doing so, Ali challenged Americans to accept what was unfamiliar to them. Ali became a social activist, speaking out on behalf of Muslims worldwide.

OTHER NOTABLE TRADITIONS AND WORLDVIEWS

In the previous sections of this book, we explored the five religions that have been most influential in the world. These religions are observed by 80 percent of the global population. The remaining 20 percent of the world follows other religious or spiritual traditions, or none at all. The next section of this book explores five of these religious, spiritual, or secular worldviews that shape the lives of many people in today's world.

Shamanism

Shamanism is a spiritual practice characterized by belief in spirits, spirit worlds, and the powers of shamans. A shaman is a person who is believed to have access to spirit worlds.

Shamanism is sometimes referred to as the "oldest religion" or the "original religion." It originated ten thousand years ago in ancient Siberian tribes. Other ancient native cultures with similar practices have also been considered shamanistic.

Today, many Indigenous groups around the world follow shamanistic practices, which vary from culture to culture. These groups are found in North and South America, East and Southeast Asia, and Oceania. Shamanism is also sometimes practiced alongside other religious traditions, such as Buddhism and Christianity.

FUN FACT

Some Hmong people, members of an ethnic group originally from Southeast Asia, practice a form of shamanism. According to Hmong tradition, a deceased person's soul must return to its birthplace before uniting with ancestors in the afterlife. Traditional Hmong funerals can last several days and involve elaborate rituals to help guide the souls of the dead to safety.

Shamans

Central to shamanistic cultures are figures called shamans. The word *shaman* originated in the Tungus tribe in Siberia. It is based on the term *saman*, meaning "one who knows." A shaman is a person who is believed to be called by spirits to take on the role of healer, counselor, and spiritual advisor of a tribal community. This calling is often said to come during a near-death experience or serious illness.

Shaman abilities vary across cultures. However, shamans are generally believed to be capable of healing the sick, communicating with spirits, and escorting the dead to the spirit world. Shamans are also sometimes said to perceive events occurring elsewhere in time and space.

One way that shamans are believed to communicate with spirits is by going into a trance, or sleeplike state. During a trance, the shaman's soul is said to travel to the spirit world. A shaman may also become possessed by a spirit during a trance. This allows the spirit to speak through the shaman.

Native American Spirituality

Native Americans are the Indigenous groups of North and South America. These groups can be traced back at least thirteen thousand years. Their traditions and ways of life came under threat with the arrival of European colonists. Many languages, rituals, and oral narratives were lost. Today, many Native American communities try to keep alive the traditions of their ancestors.

Native Americans do not describe their spiritual ways of life as "religions." In fact, the term *religion* does not have a direct translation in Native American languages. There is also no single Native American spirituality. Spiritual traditions vary greatly across tribes. However, certain characteristics are common across many Indigenous groups.

Most Native traditions are based on oral narratives, or stories told over generations. These stories often tell of humans communicating with nonhuman beings, such as spirits. Such narratives inform a common belief in the spirit world and its interaction with beings on earth.

Many Native traditions consider dreams to be portals into other worlds or realms. Dreams bring opportunities to communicate with the spirits of ancestors, animals, and others who inhabit these other realms.

FUN FACT

Sweat lodge ceremonies are common to many Native American tribes. This ceremony takes place within a domed structure covered in blankets and tarps. Inside, water is poured over hot stones to create steam. The steam is meant to heal and purify those inside the lodge.

North American tribes may refer to the Great Spirit, a supreme guide symbolized by the circle. This basic shape carries importance because of its prevalence in nature. For example, the sun and moon are circular, as is the rotation of the seasons. North American tribes also honor the complementary pairs found in nature, such as darkness and light, hot and cold, female and male.

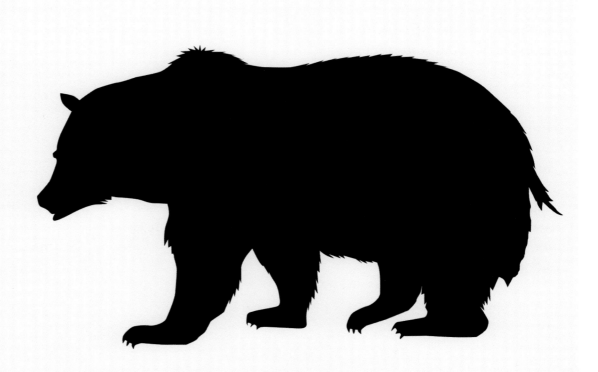

Native spiritualities commonly consider all parts of the natural world—including animals, plants, lakes, and mountains—to be sacred. Rituals often honor the relationships between living humans and these other spiritual entities. Music and dance play important roles in Native American rituals.

Sikhism

Sikhism is a monotheistic religion that began about five hundred years ago in the Punjab region in South Asia. This region includes parts of what are now Pakistan and India.

The founder of Sikhism was Guru Nanak. *Guru* means teacher. Guru Nanak's teachings drew from both Hindu and Islamic philosophies. He preached that there is one God and that everyone is equal before God.

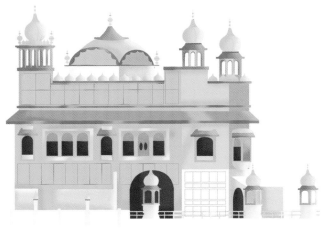

After Nanak's death, a succession of nine other gurus continued preaching Sikhism. The tenth one, Guru Gobind Singh, decided he was the last living guru. After him, the Sikh holy book would provide guidance to followers. The book, called Guru Granth Sahib, is a collection of writings by former gurus.

Today, most Sikhs live in India. They follow Guru Nanak's original teachings about the existence of one God and the equality of all. Sikhs believe it is important to remember God in everything they do. They also believe in doing work that serves others and helps society.

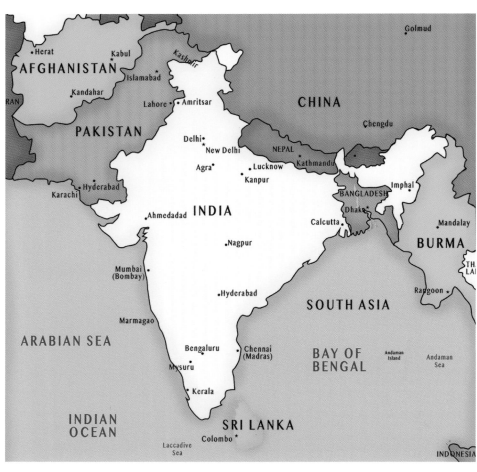

Sikhs worship in temples called gurdwaras. *Gurdwara* means "gateway to the guru." During a service, Sikhs listen to the teachings of the Guru Granth Sahib. Afterward, everyone is welcome to a meal called *langar*. Attendees sit on the floor to eat, and everyone receives the same food in equal measure. This ritual meal is a symbol of the equality of all people.

THE FIVE K'S

Members of the Sikh community must adopt the Five Ks. These are identifiers that start with the letter *K* in the Punjabi language.

KESH
uncut hair

KANGA
a wooden comb

KIRPAN
a ceremonial sword

KARA
a steel wristband

KACHERA
cotton shorts worn as undergarments

FUN FACT

Sikh men wrap their heads in long pieces of cloth called *turbans*. Sikh women traditionally wear headscarves called chunnis. Turbans and *chunnis* are symbols of Sikh pride and identity.

Taoism (or Daoism)

Taoism is an ancient philosophy and religious belief that originated in China more than two thousand years ago. Central to Taoism is the *Tao*, or "the Way." The Tao can be described as the ultimate reality in which all things are connected. Taoism is often practiced alongside Chinese folk religion. Some people blend the practices of Taoism, Buddhism, and Confucianism.

A figure called Lao Tzu is traditionally considered the founder of Taoism and writer of a text called the Tao Te Ching. However, modern scholars believe the Tao Te Ching was written by many different wise people. This text describes the nature of the universe. Taoists look to the Tao Te Ching for guidance.

Important concepts in the Tao Te Ching and Taoist philosophy are harmony and balance. For example, Taoism embraces the principle of natural and complementary forces, known as **yin and yang**. Darkness and light, action and inaction, warm and cold—these are all examples of complementary forces. Though these forces are considered opposites, Taoists believe they work together in harmony.

FUN FACT

Tai chi is a Chinese martial art associated with Taoism. It features slow, circular movements that mimic the flow of nature and the circulation of blood in the body. Modern versions of tai chi are practiced as a sport. There are even international tai chi competitions!

Taoists seek to unite with the Tao. They take part in a number of practices believed to bring one closer to the Tao. Meditation is one such practice. Taoists meditate in temples. Other temple rituals include reading scriptures, chanting prayers, and worshipping deities.

Secular Humanism

Secularism is a worldview that places focus and importance on life on earth rather than the supernatural or divine. Humanism is a worldview that emphasizes the importance of human life and human action. Secular humanism combines these two philosophies.

Some secular humanists do not believe in a God or gods. This denial of divine existence is called atheism. Other secular humanists are agnostic. This means they neither believe in nor deny divine existence, because they consider this existence to be unknowable. Whether atheist or agnostic or somewhere in between, secular humanists see the value in focusing on what they do believe in rather than what they do not believe in.

At the core of secular humanism is a belief in the goodness of humanity. Because of this, secular humanists argue that people can live ethical and meaningful lives without belief in the divine. Secular humanists put their faith in the powers of human compassion, cooperation, and ingenuity. They look to science, art, philosophy, and more as guides in deciding what is true and right.

Various groups have documented the general beliefs and goals of secular humanism. The first Humanist Manifesto was composed in 1933. The most recent manifesto was created in 2003 by members of the American Humanist Association. It discusses the importance of observation, experimentation, and rational analysis in gaining knowledge of the world. It also stresses the value of human welfare, community, and equality. Secular humanists assert that the responsibility to build a world based on these ideals falls on humans alone.

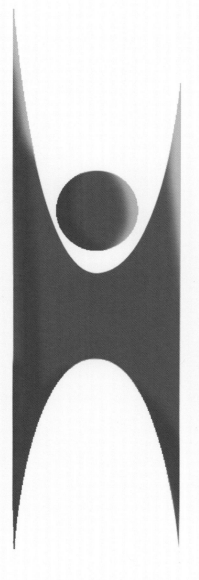

FUN FACT

Sunday Assembly is a secular gathering open to all individuals. The first Sunday Assembly took place in 2013 in London, England. It has since inspired the establishment of more than forty-five Sunday Assembly chapters in eight different countries. These events celebrate life through songs, readings, and inspiring speeches. In some ways, these gatherings mirror the congregations of many religious traditions. However, Sunday Assembly does not include doctrine (a set of ideas or beliefs that are taught or believed to be true) or mention of God.

EMPATHY

I will consider other people's thoughts, feelings and experiences.

CRITICAL THINKING

I will practice good judgment by asking questions and thinking for myself.

ETHICAL DEVELOPMENT

I will always focus on becoming a better person.

RESPONSIBILITY

I will be a good person—even when no one is looking—and own the consequences of my actions.

THE
TEN
COMMITMENTS
LIVING HUMANIST VALUES

PEACE & SOCIAL JUSTICE

I will help people solve problems and handle disagreements in ways that are fair for everyone.

GLOBAL AWARENESS

I will be a good neighbor to the people who share the Earth with me and help make the world a better place for everyone.

SERVICE & PARTICIPATION

I will help my community in ways that let me get to know the people I'm helping.

ENVIRONMENTALISM

I will take care of the Earth and the life on it.

HUMILITY

I will be aware of my strengths and weaknesses, and appreciate the strengths and weaknesses of others.

ALTRUISM

I will help others in need without hoping for rewards.

INTERFAITH FAMILIES

Many people practice a single faith tradition within their family. But many others grow up observing more than one religious or spiritual tradition. This often happens when two parents from different faith backgrounds decide to teach their kids about both traditions. Families that embrace more than one faith tradition are known as interfaith families.

· ·

Growing Up "Muslic"

Jehan Elsagher used to call herself "Muslic." That's because her father was Muslim and her mother Catholic. Jehan grew up practicing both religions.

"I was proud to call myself a Muslic. I had the pleasure of practicing both religions and learning about both of my parents' faith backgrounds."

Jehan grew up attending both a mosque and a church. She fasted during Ramadan and also observed the season of Lent. Her family celebrated both the Islamic festival of Eid and the Christian holiday of Christmas.

"My parents raised us to be very open-minded."

While Jehan was proud of her upbringing in two faiths, she struggled to feel like she fully belonged to either. As an adult, Jehan decided to be baptized as a Christian. In doing so, she became an official member of her church community.

"Although I am now Christian, I will always be grateful for how I was raised, and I will continue to support my dad in his religious faith."

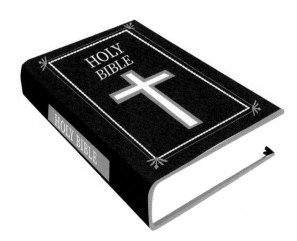

Jewish and Catholic

Leslie Joseph grew up in a Jewish family. Her husband, Mark Lybik, was brought up in a Catholic family. Leslie wanted to pass down the Jewish tradition to her own kids. However, she and Mark also wanted their kids to have an understanding of Catholic traditions. So, Leslie and Mark decided to raise their kids Jewish while also taking part in Christian holiday traditions.

"We made a deal that whenever it was possible, we would celebrate Christmas and Easter with our Catholic family in Michigan."

Leslie and Mark's three sons grew up going to the synagogue, Hebrew school, and Jewish summer camp. They each had a bar mitzvah when they were thirteen years old, and they celebrated Jewish holidays. But most years, they also celebrated Christian holidays—especially Christmas—with their Catholic relatives. They gathered for meals, exchanged gifts, and occasionally attended church services.

"We hoped that by exposing them to both Judaism and Catholicism, they'd have a deep appreciation for both religions and cultures."

INTERFAITH ACTION

Just as there are interfaith families, there are also interfaith communities and organizations. These groups promote positive, cooperative interaction between individuals of diverse faith backgrounds. Interfaith organizations work to address global issues such as poverty, climate change, and racism. They believe in the power of joining forces to create positive change.

Parliament of the World's Religions

In 1893, spiritual leaders from around the world traveled to Chicago, Illinois. They were attending the first formal gathering of representatives of Eastern and Western spiritual traditions. The gathering, organized by John Henry Barrows, became known as the Parliament of World's Religions. Several thousand attendees listened to speeches from representatives of Hinduism, Buddhism, Islam, and more. The event is considered the birth of a global interfaith movement.

Today, the Parliament of the World's Religions is the largest interfaith event in the world. It takes place every few years with the goal to promote harmony across the world's religions. Organizers of the Parliament believe this interfaith harmony is critical to transforming the world for the better.

Interfaith Youth Core

Interfaith Youth Core (IFYC) is a national nonprofit organization founded in 2002. The organization is built on the belief that people of different faiths, worldviews, and traditions can find common values. The founder of IFYC, Eboo Patel, grew up in a Muslim family that had immigrated to the United States from India. As a college student, Patel imagined an interfaith movement of young people using their shared values to work toward common goals.

Based in Chicago, Illinois, IFYC has worked with hundreds of US colleges and universities to set up interfaith groups and organize service projects. IFYC also trains students and educators in interfaith cooperation and leadership. In doing so, IFYC equips rising leaders to successfully navigate religious diversity in the twenty-first century.

Women of Liberia Mass Action for Peace

In 2003, a coalition of Christian and Muslim women engaged in nonviolent protest to end a fourteen-year civil war in Liberia. Liberian peace activist Leymah Gbowee led this interfaith movement known as the Women of Liberia Mass Action for Peace.

Under Gbowee's leadership, thousands participated in public protests, pressuring Liberia's president to take part in formal peace talks. Gbowee and nearly two hundred other women also formed a human barricade to stop officials from leaving the peace talks until they had reached an agreement. This interfaith effort led to the signing of a peace treaty and the eventual election of Ellen Johnson Sirleaf as president of Liberia.

In 2011, Gbowee was awarded the Nobel Peace Prize. She shared the prize with two other women, including Ellen Johnson Sirleaf.

CONCLUSION

What have you learned from your tour of religions around the world? You probably became familiar with religions you hadn't heard of. Maybe you picked up new knowledge about your own religious tradition. And perhaps you've come to appreciate the many differences—as well as the similarities—across religions.

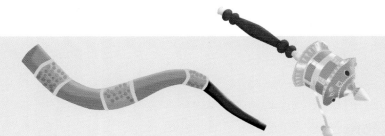

Religions Are Diverse

Think about the different beliefs you have encountered in this book. The Jewish tradition worships one God; Hindus believe the divine is manifested in many gods and goddesses; secular humanists maintain that God is not necessary to live a meaningful life. The religions of the world are wonderfully diverse in their beliefs and ways of understanding reality.

Diversity also exists *within* every religious tradition. Members of the same religion often differ in how they view their faith. This shows that each individual has a unique relationship to the divine or ultimate reality. As a famous Taoist quote puts it, "The Tao has ten thousand gates . . . and it is up to each of us to find our own."

Religions Are Similar

While religions can differ greatly in their beliefs, practices, and rituals, they also have a lot in common. All religions and other worldviews give their followers a sense of meaning and purpose. They also seek to provide answers about what realities lie beyond this world.

At the same time, faith traditions seek to answer the question of how we should live together in this world. Most religions and worldviews promote some form of "golden rule." This is a principle of treating others as you would want to be treated.

Every tradition holds up role models who exemplify the golden rule by serving those in need or advocating for human rights. Members of different traditions can also come together to live out this golden rule. This interfaith action demonstrates that community and compassion are central to the human experience.

Keep Exploring

We hope your interest in religions around the world does not end with this book. There is so much more to learn! Challenge yourself to follow some of the suggestions for exploring more about these traditions. Find a neighbor and interview them about their faith tradition. Go to a religious service with a friend who follows a practice that's different from your own. Whatever you do, remember to respect others' beliefs, appreciate different traditions, and stay curious!

BIOS

Sonja Hagander is an ordained clergy in the Evangelical Lutheran Church in America. She has held various leadership roles in higher education and congregational life and developed and led valuable inter-religious programs in university and community settings, including educational travel experiences for students, professors, clergy, and laity to Palestine, Israel, and Norway, and disaster response efforts in various parts of the United States. Sonja is a contributor to the book *Faith in Action: A Handbook for Activists, Advocates, and Allies* (Fortress Press). She lives with her family in the Twin Cities.

Matthew Maruggi is an Associate Professor of Religion at Augsburg University, where he teaches and researches in the areas of vocation, spirituality, the ethics of world religions, and interfaith studies. Matthew co-directs the Interfaith Scholar Seminar, promoting interfaith dialogue and community engagement with students from a variety of backgrounds. He lives in Minneapolis, Minnesota, with his family.

Megan Borgert-Spaniol is a children's book author who likes to write with a pastry by her side. Megan lives in Minneapolis, Minnesota, with a tall goofy man and small chatty cat.

Chester Bentley was interested in illustration and art from a young age. In school, he could always be found sketching something during lunchtime. Chester studied at Art College and has worked in illustration ever since. A highly skilled and versatile artist, he thrives on new challenges and works with a variety of media.